The Trial of Dr Luther

The Trial of Dr Luther

A Play

by

Oliver McQuillan

ISBN 978-0-9575967-1-9

The Palmerston Press
40 Palmerston Road
Dublin 6
Ireland

e-mail: omcquillan@mcq.ie

The Trial of Dr Luther was first produced in the New Theatre, Dublin, on Monday, 31 October 2011.

The part of Martin Luther was performed by Oliver McQuillan.

It was produced and directed by Peter Reid.

Scene 1

Night. A small cell-like room in a fourteenth century German house. Spartan, a simple desk, drapes over a doorway. A lute with broken strings sits on a shelf, an oil lamp gutters. A woodcut of the Crucifixion by a German master. A prie dieu.

A bulky figure sleeps at the desk.

Three loud knocks on a heavy door. Pause. The figure stirs. Knocks again. He sits up. It is Martin Luther, now in old age. He is dressed heavily against the cold.

LUTHER: Who's there? (*More curiosity than fear. He peers into the darkness.*) Who's there? (*Takes up stick.*) Are you going to hide yourself in the shadows? (*He gets up awkwardly, moves slowly towards his Visitor. Peers closely but without recognition.*) Have I met you before? (*Smiles, drily.*) Perhaps ... in my cell in the Fortress of Wartburg, you pestered me there one night? (*Pause.*) The same spirit of melancholy (*sniffs*) the same odour of decay, hangs over you. Yes, I remember. If it is you, I threw my inkpot at you once. I missed.

Well? Has my time come?

(*He walks slowly back to the wall where the Crucifixion scene hangs. Kneels on prie dieu.*)

Oh Heavenly Father, if I am to leave this body now and be torn away from this life, yet I have certain knowledge that I shall remain with Thee forever and no one can tear me from Thy hands. Amen.

I am ready.

(*He goes to a chair on which lie a greatcoat and doctor's hat. He puts them on. Turns to Visitor. Pause.*)

Still not a word. Are you come to mock me? Or do you wish to question me? Is that why you are here? You want to confront me with my sins? My numberless failings? I am not afraid. Christ absolves me of all of them, only he can. I am beyond fear. I live now with the certainty that I am saved, not by anything I have done or who I am, but by God's grace alone, through my faith in his son, Christ our Lord.

(*Pain. He leans on desk, breathing heavily.*)

Will you taunt me with my infirmities? Save your breath. I have had gallstones, sciatica, gout, varicose veins, haemorrhoids, bad circulation, high blood pressure. Arthritis. Kidney disease. Constipation. Take your pick. I won't run away. When Death comes I am ready to greet him as a friend. (*He looks again.*) Oh ... and of the two eyes God gave me, only one serves me still. When death comes ... (*hopeful*) I am ready to greet him as a friend ... Death, my friend? (*Peers again.*) No? No.

No. Get thee behind me. Christ will defend me always. And if that is not good enough for you Satan, I have also shit and pissed. Wipe your mouth on that and stuff yourself full with it.

Still tongue-tied? What can I say if you will not speak to me, question me? By your silence you would like to scratch at my conscience in my final moments as a beggar scratches at a scab? Scratch away. Which scab first? Which of Martin Luther's sores would you like to make me gaze again at in despair before I go? I know what men said - still say - about me. My terrible anger. My lack of charity. My pride. Yes?

What anger? Rage. Rage against that Anti-Christ the pope in Rome. What lack of charity? For those who would use religious fear to extort money from the poor? My anger at the peasants - whom some say I betrayed? I condemned equally those miserable wretches for their atrocities during their uprising and the noblemen for their brutal reprisals afterwards. My pride? That I dared stand alone against the might of the Church and bear witness to God's truth as revealed in the Bible?

Or am I to be accused again of taking away from the people the comfort of their relics, their superstitions? Their simple faith in indulgences?

Indulgences. Yes. People have forgotten now that in those days everyone was complaining about indulgences. I was a devout monk, a preacher in the monastery, fresh from my studies as a young doctor in theology, passionately immersed in the Holy Scriptures. Even I didn't know what indulgences were. No one knew what they were.

Should I have remained silent?

It was only when Cheap Jack Tetzel came rattling his money box for Rome that I began to look seriously into the abuse of indulgences and tried to start a debate about them. People came to me in confession, told me of the sermons preached by the Dominican charlatan. Amazing stories of the impressive pomp with which he made his appearances. The ringing of bells; the public receptions; the large red cross erected in the church between two red banners emblazoned with the pope's arms. The carriage festooned with letters of indulgence in which Tetzel drove past. Salvation for sale. Nobody in authority complained. The bishops and the doctors held their peace. No one was prepared to bell the cat, for one simple reason: the Dominicans held the threat of burning at the stake over all of us.

But I spoke out. Through foolishness, you will say? Through pride you will say?

I can tell you I did not enjoy the fame it brought me. The song was pitched too high for my voice.

And I was naive. The preacher on indulgences was the direct representative of the pope. To attack indulgences was to attack the authority of the pope.

Was I God's fool then? Perhaps. All that was a long time ago. And I was a mere monk ...

But even that had come about by accident.

When I was in the university of Erfurt, the study of theology was far from my mind. Erfurt was a metropolis where philosophy was more important than theology. It was a turbulent place even then, and would support me later when my struggle began.

It was there I held a bible in my hands for the first time. But I didn't look at it much. They had only one copy, and it was chained to a desk.

I was very happy, happy to be away from the harsh discipline of my childhood. Yes. When I was a small, if I as much as sneaked a nut my poor mother would beat me black and blue. Once my father thrashed me so severely that I ran away. I brought up our own children differently. Kate will testify to that. Too little discipline perhaps.

At school a new era of beating began. Mansfeld, where we grew up, had a grammar school which was an asses' stable and devil's school run by tyrants and jailers, a hell and purgatory in one. On one single morning the master birched me fifteen times. Everything was in Latin, German was forbidden.

Then to Eisenach. I loved Eisenach and the parish school there. The days of the birch were over. I was a happy boy, and we would go around singing, collecting tiny gifts of alms. It was there I experienced an act of great kindness. I had relations in the town who were known to be too poor to afford to keep me. One day I was singing with other boys outside the house of the Cotta family. Frau Cotta loved music and took an instant liking to my singing. There and then she offered me lodgings without charge. Dear Frau Cotta. I have never forgotten her generosity and her kindness to a fourteen year old boy far away from home.

All my life music has been the art closest to me. When I was a student they used to call me 'the musician'.

(*He touches the lax strings of the lute.*)

Silent now. Silent now.

(*Pause.*)

Where was I? Yes. I became a monk. I was twenty two. I was returning to the university one night when a violent storm broke out. A flash of lightening threw me to the ground. In my terror I prayed to St Anne.

"Help me, St Anne; help me and I will become a monk."

And that was it. My student days were over. I returned to the university, sold all my law books. The night I left I held a magnificent dinner for my friends. They were all scholars, modest and virtuous girls among them. We had an evening filled with joy, and as usual I entertained them, singing and playing my lute. When it was over they thanked me and left, not knowing what I intended to do.

That night I became a monk.

Of course I was disobeying my father for the first time in my life. "Despair is the making of a monk." I tried to explain that to him. He didn't understand. He had set his heart on my becoming a lawyer.

It was to be a long time before we were reconciled.

(*He comes forward again, looks at his Visitor.*)

Hmnn. You neither smile nor frown at me. What is it you want to hear about old Luther? Questions for the hours of darkness. The questions that torment me as I lie awake. Was there ever *any* love in my heart? Or was there room only for wrath? Was I happy with my decision to follow Christ, made, like St Paul's, on impulse? Do I feel pain, even now, remorse at the divisions I have brought to God's people? When I see how little they have changed in their hearts?

Am I to admit, finally, that I am weary, ready to return home? Is that what you want to hear?

Was there ever love in my heart?

I'll give you the answer.

I lived as a blameless Augustinian monk in Wittenberg. See him there, the young man filled with the fear of God. At his shoulder stands Father Staupitz the Prior.

He was a real father to me.

When he saw my fear of God's wrath he told me God was not angry with me, I was angry with God. When I wailed about my sins he laughed and said I hadn't committed any sins at all. Real sins were to murder your parents, to blaspheme in public, to scorn God, to commit adultery and so on.

"If Christ is to help you," he said, "you must keep a list of real, honest-to-goodness sins and not go hobbling around nursing toy ones, imagining you've committed a sin every time you fart!"

That was love.

Yet I had an uneasy conscience that I was a sinner before God, unable to be reconciled through anything I myself could do. Not only did I not love – no, I hated the just God who punishes sinners. I wrestled fiercely with that passage in St Paul which I so ardently desired to understand: "The just man shall live by faith." I spent days and nights thinking of nothing else.

The just man shall live by faith.

I had been allocated a small room in a tower in the monastery. There, at the age of thirty I at last had a room of my own where I could work undisturbed. It has remained my working place to this day.

I was very busy, both as university lecturer and a pastor. Teaching. Preaching. Everything I have done since has been rooted in these two offices. When the devil (*smiles, looks at Visitor*) whispered to me "you have not been called, you have no vocation", I comforted myself with the thought that I was now a doctor of

Sacred Scripture and bound by my doctor's oath to teach the scriptures, whether I was worthy or not.

And so the devil was the father of my theology. Had it not been for these temptations I would never have come to the knowledge of God's grace.

I agonised endlessly over the problem of God's forgiving mercy. Was I damned because I was a sinner or could I gain salvation? Must I remain in fear to the end of my life? I turned to St Paul and St Augustine for answers to the questions which burned inside me. What was this grace, this gift of God, the door to salvation?

Finally God had mercy on me, and I came to understand the meaning of those words, namely: salvation is a gift of God which we gain through faith in his Son, Jesus Christ. "The just man shall live by faith". It was so simple. Faith. We are all sinners through original sin, but I now saw that the sinner is justified by faith alone, on the authority of scripture alone; that we are saved from our sins by God's grace alone, through faith alone.

It was then I understood that I had been completely born again and that I had stepped through the open gates of paradise itself. St Paul had given me the answer to the question: is grace in the good works we do, which give us the satisfied feeling that we have done all that was required of us? No. Did the Church attach too much importance to such outward signs? Yes.

It became clear to me that abuses had crept in. The abuse of indulgences, for example, whereby the forgiveness of sins could be bought with money instead of being earned by sincere penitence. Naively, I also believed all I needed to do was to point this out to the proper authorities and it would be corrected.

So I wrote about indulgences in modest and reverential language to the Archbishop of Mainz and to other high prelates.

Looking back, I sometimes ask myself: how did a debate about the right means of salvation and a return to the Gospel of Jesus Christ develop into a confrontation between a monk and the might of the Church over the authority and infallibility of the Pope?

Not long after I was ordained my order sent me to Rome on a mission. When I first arrived in the Eternal City I was almost sorry my parents were still alive because the huge indulgence my visit earned could have made them instantly happy in the life beyond. The indulgences one could buy back in Germany were paltry compared with those available in Rome. My great wish was to free my grandfather from purgatory. All I had to do, I was told, was to ascend a certain stone staircase, the Scala Sancta, on my knees, saying an Our Father on each step. When I reached the top I was informed I had just come up the very steps Jesus had climbed to Pilate' s palace. "Pilate's palace? Rome? But Pilate's palace was in Jerusalem," I said. "Oh no", I was told."After the destruction of Jerusalem those heavy stone steps had been carried all the way from Jerusalem to Rome. By angels."

I was also supposed to say Mass in the Lateran but it was always too crowded and I couldn't get near an altar. So I sat outside and ate a pickled herring instead.

I don't remember much about St Peter's. It was just a vast building site. All I remember are some curiosities: the rope with which Judas hanged himself; a stone with a furrow as broad as a man's finger caused by the tears St Peter shed after he had denied Christ. Through my work I also learned who Rome's two pre-eminent saints were, without whose intercession nothing could be achieved: Saint Golden Coin and Saint Silver Piece.

Back in Wittenberg I shouldn't have been so surprised when Tetzel came marching through the countryside banging his drum to raise funds for the building of St Peter's. A Dominican - what else - Tetzel demanded and got a salary twenty times that of a university professor and was paid expenses.

"I have received such dispensation from the pope" he shouted, "that even if you were to have raped the Virgin Mary and got her with child I could grant you forgiveness, provided you put a suitable contribution in my box".

A believable story. For his gullible listeners he painted a picture of dead souls languishing in the agonies of purgatory crying out for relief.

"The dead call out, 'Save us! Save us! We are in dire torment from which you can redeem us for a pittance. Will you leave our souls in flames? Will you delay our promised glory?' As soon as the coin in the coffer rings, out a soul from purgatory springs. Will you not then for a mere quarter florin buy one of my letters of indulgence and send an immortal soul instantly to heaven."

As soon as the coin in the coffer rings, out a soul from purgatory springs.

And so I wrote my theses.

People sometimes ask me, did I actually take a hammer and nail them to the door of the castle church? So appropriately, on the Eve of the feast of All Saints?

Sometimes a story takes hold of people's minds, becomes so powerful, it is transformed into the truth. But Melanchthon says I did. That was how we did it in those days.

For two weeks after they appeared there was a deathly silence. No one seemed interested. So I sent a copy to a few friends. Remember, these were merely debating points for academic disputation among scholars.

But no. They were shouted from the rooftops. Within a fortnight my ninety-five theses on the abuse of indulgences had spread through the length and breadth of Germany. Why such interest? Because everyone was complaining about indulgences. I was astonished. If they had wanted a criticism of indulgences I could have written a proper one, but that wasn't my purpose. Look at the theses. Read them. Mere talking points, not established truths. I had no blow against the Church in mind. Yes, I wanted to see it reformed. But I certainly had no intention of leaving it.

But very soon I realised that what I was doing was no less than trying to storm heaven itself and set the world on fire. And I was afraid. Again, the song was trying to go too high for my voice.

When I wrote that first letter to Archbishop Albrecht of Mainz I didn't know this was the document which would mark the start of the great battle of my life. A year later I wrote to the pope himself and found myself summoned to Augsburg to answer to the great Cardinal Cajetan. Augsburg, in the heart of Catholic Bavaria.

From Wittenberg to Augsburg is over three hundred miles. I made the journey on foot, not a penny in my pocket, my habit threadbare. In mortal fear because I faced my enemies alone.

In every Augustinian monastery I stayed in on the way they warned me:

"They will burn you. Turn back." "Remember Jan Hus", they said.

Poor Jan Hus. His treatment was indeed a warning to me. He had been given safe conduct to attend the Council of Constance. But despite their promises they burned him there. As I pondered his fate I realised that I too faced death at the stake.

Cardinal Cajetan had nothing but contempt for me. A "fratellino", he called me. A shabby little friar. Even though as a Dominican he had taken a vow of poverty himself. He didn't understand indulgences either, but it was dogma and not open to question. For him the solution to the problem was easy. All I had to do was to say that simple word of three syllables: *revoco.* I recant.

"My dear son", Cajetan called me. "The pope is above the councils and above the scriptures too. I am authorised to pronounce excommunication on you and on all who take your part and to lay all those places that shelter you under the interdict. Recant!"

I turned to go. He shouted again:

"Recant!"

I didn't know it then ... this was the moment that marked my break with the Church and the Church's break with me.

What was I? A university lecturer who had almost lost his job. A lowly mendicant friar in the eyes of the authorities in Rome. Someone to be burned. Quickly. *Quam celerrime.*

I had to escape. It was clear that they planned to drag me off to Rome in chains. My friend Father Staupitz found a horse for me, and with time only to put on my cowl and cloak – no shoes even - I left the city secretly and fled to Coburg. There was nowhere safe to hide there either, so my poor old nag had to stumble on another two hundred miles to Wittenberg.

They raged. And the more they raged, the bigger my strides. I marched on from my first position on indulgences, they yapped at my heels. I moved on to the next, the authority of the pope, and they yapped at me there. I began to preach against excommunication.

Next to indulgences, excommunication was one of the most universally deplored scandals. Fear of it was greater than the fear of purgatory. This weapon of the Church, once reserved for great and important cases, now threatened everyone from the richest to the poorest, the poor much more than the great. It had even become an easy and widespread means of raising taxes. Excommunication, like indulgences, had become an instrument of terror, a means of controlling people, a way of extorting money.

For me all that mattered were faith and scripture. No one could come between a man's conscience and his God.

I wrote to the pope three times. The first time I threw myself at his feet. In the second letter a year later I called myself his humble servant, but refused to recant. In the third I addressed him as an equal and pitied him as a poor Daniel in the den of lions which was the Vatican. I told the truth, that the pope was called the vicar of Christ because a vicar was someone who was present when someone more important was absent. In the case of Rome it was Christ who was absent.

When they opposed what I saw as inescapably true I carried my criticisms further and further, until one day I woke up and found to my astonishment that I had irrevocably broken with popery.

"Foxes have arisen", they wrote, "seeking to destroy the vineyard. The wild boar from the forest seeks to destroy it".

Exsurge Domine. A Papal Bull to teach Christians the evil of Doctor Luther. Forty one errors, they said.

"A wild boar has entered thy vineyard, O Lord" Pope Leo thundered. His Holiness cared as little for wild boar Luther as he did for the vineyard I was said to be invading. That pleasure-loving pope prized only one hunt - that for the real wild boars he chased in the forests outside Rome. Wild boar Luther he left to his theologian Doctor Eck to hunt down.

Eck branded me a follower of Jan Hus ... remember the flames?

When the Papal Bull arrived in Wittenberg I marched with the other professors to the carrion pit outside the city gates where a bonfire was ready. John Agricola threw in the volumes of Canon Law, the Decretals, and on top of these the Summa of Thomas Aquinas.

We had started with the Decretals, that corrupt body of legislation introduced by the papacy over centuries as Canon Law, because they were the base on which the institutional Church of Rome and the papacy were grounded. Laws which were a purely human institution. And yet through this Canon Law, a swamp of heresies, the pope had placed himself above the Scriptures, above the word of God. He had to account to no one, and claimed to be infallible and irremovable, however great his offence. Canon law also allowed the papacy to claim to be superior to all secular law.

I watched these books burn and quietly dropped the Papal Bull into the flames. As it caught fire the smell of scorching papal flesh spread across Christendom. There was no turning back. That flesh was to have been Martin Luther. Instead, the smell which wafted over Europe was the stench of Roman corruption going up in flames.

(He turns to look at his Visitor again. There is no one there. He moves closer, peering through the darkness.)

Are you still there? Is this the end then?

Are you trying to make me feel fear? I have already faced death at the stake not once, but twice. Now all I face is my eternal reward.

(*He walks to picture of Christ.*)

Agnus Dei, qui tollis peccata mundi.

Sweet Latin. Am I to turn to you now at the end? They have forgotten that you were the language of my struggle. Of my Theses. My beloved translation of the Bible into German was your offspring.

(*Sings*) *Dona nobis pacem.*

Ah, Josquin, how I miss those words.

And so long since I heard your music floating like angels wings. Banished from Wittenberg, never to be heard again this side of the grave.

(*He is lost in thought. We hear the Agnus Dei from Josquin's* L'Homme Armé Mass.)

When the angel choirs stand before the Lord God, they will sing with your sweet voice, Josquin, and you and I, my friend, will join the singing.

(*Sings. Then kneels. The music continues.*)

Dear Josquin, I am to follow you now. May the Lord have mercy. Grant me rest.

Light fades. End of scene one.

Scene 2

(*Luther is still on his knees. We hear the hymn* Von Himmel Hoch *sung by children's voices. He wakens slowly, straightens up, puzzled delight, as in a dream. Stands.*)

LUTHER: My hymn for the feast of the Christ Child? Christmas. The happiest feast of the year, when God sent his son to be one of us.

Kate and our little ones around the tree. Hans, our first-born. Magdalena, still with us then. I wrote this hymn for you when the angels took you from us. Little Martin. Paul. Margaret. Elizabeth. Elizabeth. (*Pause.*) Poor Elizabeth. Gone already from this vale of tears at only eight months in age, taken by the kind Lord to his bosom.

(*He sings, wordless, along with the music. It fades.*)

(*Softly, pain*) Oh Kate ...

(*He looks around.*)

Kate? (*Louder*) Kate! This is not my room. Where am I? Not the Fortress of Wartburg ... No ... (*Looks out window.*) Eisleben. Eisleben.

Oh, Kate! Kate! Am I to die alone here so far away from you?

(He peers around. Pause. Smiles, remembering. Opens locket.)

Katerina, Domina mea.

The heretic monk and his runaway nun.

Remember? Even Erasmus spread the rumour that I married you because you were pregnant. When our boy arrived after the normal interval of a year he retracted this slander.

And my father ... always so harsh in his judgements ... he only became reconciled to me when we married and presented him with a grandson. Through you I was restored to his favour, became once more his dear son.

Eisleben.

(He looks around the room, smiles.)

In my old room in the monastery I slept on a bed of straw under a blanket. Before I married I used to joke, no one had made up my bed for over a year; the straw was rotting from my sweat. I wore myself out with work during the day, so that I just fell into bed at night oblivious to everything.

Then she came into my life, my gracious Miss Catharine Luther von Bora, and Zühlsdorf, and all other titles that apply. My darling. And my preacher. And gardener. And brewer. And all things else. She ruled both her household and her husband, brought order into my life. It was a little world, ours, a simple house within the walls of the old monastery. Not very romantic.

Until we married I had still been wearing the monk's habit, long after everyone else had given it up. (*Remembers.*) For seven years after I posted my Theses. Living as a monk still, but without following the rules of the order.

And then marriage? I had preached the end of celibacy. Many of my clerical colleagues in Wittenberg had wives by then. Now they urged me to practise what I preached.

At my request, a friend of mine, a merchant, had undertaken to help twelve young nuns escape from a convent. He smuggled them out in his covered wagon, hidden among fish barrels. When they arrived in Wittenberg we lodged them in the old cloister. Within two years we had found homes, husbands or employment for all. Except one. A rather haughty young lady – I thought - called Catherine von Bora. I approached a number of suitors on her behalf, but without success. Then I heard she had said she would be prepared to marry me. She was twenty six, I was forty two. We married.

I knew of the popular superstition that the only offspring of the sacrilegious union of a monk and a nun could be a two-headed monster. People waited. When Kate became pregnant there were anxious months ahead. But our little boy arrived without defects, a healthy, hungry, thirsty little fellow. And only one head.

There is no sweeter thing than the love of a woman. And no greater gift of God than the birth of a child. My Kate, the morning star of Wittenberg, bore six children, three boys and three girls. Two of the girls died and there was a miscarriage. But, the oldest boy, Hans, is now a strapping nineteen-year-old, and little Margaret, the youngest, is eleven.

Man and woman were created by God to grow and multiply. Rome thought otherwise. There were eighteen Papal legal impediments to marriage, but if you had money you could buy a dispensation from any one of them. When I married, Rome, which crawled with the mistresses and bastard children of clergy, screamed that I had broken my vow.

During my time as a student in Erfurt the canons' mistresses used to parade through the town in their jewellery. Concubines they called them. There was a popular song of the day:

(*He sings*)

He came from Würzburg with his whore
In Erfurt now ten years or more
A canon of the church, alas
In all those years ne'er once said Mass.
In all those years ne'er once said Mass.

(*Shouts*) Do you like my song, friend? No? (*To the dark*) Ah, only silence still. (*Quietly*) There is one to whom music is alien. Satan, the spirit of gloom, he cannot bear joy. To no one is music more repugnant than to him.

And song is second only to scripture as a comfort to the human soul in sadness and temptation. The person who sings as he prays, prays twice over. God preaches his Gospel of grace through music such as that of Josquin which flows willingly, happily, sweetly, like the song of the finch. It was through music I sought consolation in my states of melancholy and doubt. Through it I saw revealed an exalted realm beyond the real one, which for most people is only wretched and dismal. I knew the magnificent compositions of the great masters of our day. Senfl - a Catholic - was my favourite. I wept when Josquin died. The world was never worthy of such masters.

Looking at me now you would never think I was a bright and lively fellow when I was young, going from house to house, singing for joy, playing my lute. Yes, music gladdens the soul.

Except perhaps just once ...

... After my break with Rome, I heard singing one day outside my window. I looked out. A group of seminarians seemed to be serenading me. I recognised the melody the piece was based on. The Te Deum. (*Sings*) *Te Deum laudamus*. We praise thee O Lord. Then I heard the words they were singing: (*sings*) *Te Lutherum Damnamus.* We damn thee, Luther. No praise there for God's servant, only damnation.

I wonder, when I die will the pope call for a universal Te Deum to be sung in thanksgiving? Probably. The hatred will live on. Erasmus said of me: "He made himself hated by seizing the pope by the tiara and the monks by their ... paunches".

Hatred. And love. I thank God there was also great love in my life. I have the love of a good wife, and I love her. And I love my children. And I love music of course.

I also love flowers. During the dispute with Eck in Leipzig, when my life was at stake, I faced my enemies wearing a small posy of flowers, carnations, attached to my habit. It was hot and crowded, and when I spoke in the debate I inhaled their perfume from time to time. The story spread that I had marched through the town in triumph garlanded with flowers.

In Leipzig that year, and later in Worms in the presence of the Emperor, I beseeched them to teach me from Holy Scripture where I was in error. But rather than enter into a religious disputation they repeated their demand that I recant. Finally the Chancellor put the question bluntly:

"Will you recant?"

I replied: "Since your Imperial Majesty and your Eminences desire a simple answer, then I will give you one, without teeth or horns: Unless I can be persuaded otherwise by the testimony of Holy Scripture and on clear reasonable grounds – for I cannot believe either in Pope or in Councils alone, since it is known that they have often erred and contradicted themselves – then I must remain faithful to those passages of Holy Scripture which I have quoted. My conscience is captive to the word of God. Therefore I neither can nor will recant anything, because to go against my conscience would endanger my salvation. Here I stand. I can do no other. So help me God. Amen".

The break was complete.

I went on to question the pope's claim to be the supreme head of Christendom. Specifically I cited the Greek church and protested against its members being called 'heretics' or even 'unbelievers', to fight and kill whom rulers had been encouraged to undertake crusades and were rewarded with indulgences for doing so.

When I learned that the so-called Donation of Constantine, the basis for the papal claim to power, whereby that emperor was said to have given the western part of his empire to the pope to rule ... when I heard that that document was an eighth century forgery my conviction was complete that the Antichrist ruled in Rome. Lies, confusion, conflict. These are the characteristics of the Antichrist. The lie about the Donation was perpetuated in Canon law.

For years there had been talk about the sinful life in Rome. Anything I was ever to say about the cesspit that was the Vatican would be as nothing compared with writings circulating in Rome at the time of my visit. That was only seven years after the death of the Borgia pope Alexander who had paraded his mistresses and children in front of the faithful outside St Peter's. "Rome crawls with vermin and vileness", I read then. I was shocked at the time, but the words stayed with me.

People waited for a *Papa Angelicus*, an "angelic pope", to appear who would put everything right. This didn't happen. Rome was a city of money-lenders, buying, selling, changing, exchanging, tippling, lying, deceiving, robbing, stealing, boasting, whoring, knaving. What else could the pope be but the Antichrist, the final disorder.

He allowed priests to live with women, forbidding only marriage. These women were known as priests' whores, the children as priests' bastards. I said that not every clergyman could live without a woman, not so much because of frailty as for the sake of order in his household. In this case he should take a wife. Next to God's word there is no more precious treasure than holy matrimony. Our body is largely the flesh of woman. There it was conceived, grew, was born, suckled and nourished, so that it is utterly impossible for us to separate ourselves from the flesh of woman, or to renounce it.

The Bible was the basis of everything I taught and preached. In the Bible I could find only one sacrament, the Word of God, and three sacramental signs: Baptism,

Penance and the Lord's Supper. To these the Church added four others. None of them is contained in Holy Scripture, and hence they are invalid.

As for the Mass, it is not a sacrifice, whereby Christ becomes a sacrificial victim again and again on the altar, and which only the priest can perform. There was only one sacrifice, that of Christ himself on Calvary. We recall this in the sacrament of the Lord's Supper. I preached the universal priesthood of all who are baptised and who believe, and in this sacrament I demanded the direct participation of each communicant who believes in Christ's words, "Do this in commemoration of me. This is my body, this is my blood".

The entire teaching system of the Church, with its doctrines and dogmas, is based on the principle that the individual must adapt himself to the whole, he cannot be left to see with his own eyes. I rejected this.

This rebellion was my decisive act, my act of temerity. It was the case the Emperor formulated against me at Worms when he sentenced me as a heretic. I knew what this meant. His grandfather the Emperor Maximilian had proclaimed: "Heretics shall suffer the death for which they long; they are to be burned alive in full view of the people and undergo the judgement of fire".

Nevertheless, at the end of the debate Emperor Charles ordered my departure from the city, and honoured my safe-conduct.

On my way back to Wittenberg Elector Frederick had me seized and spirited away to Wartburg Castle in Eisenach. There I was to remain a prisoner for my own safety, disguised as country squire Joerg, hidden behind a long curling beard. I was so long out of sight there that many thought me dead.

It was in the Wartburg that I translated the New Testament into German, to bring the word of God directly to the people. The pen is an easy implement, one needs only a goose quill and that can be picked up anywhere. Nevertheless it is the best part of the human body - the head – and the noblest member - the tongue - and the highest achievement – language - that have to be called into service and do most of the work. It is said of a writer that only three fingers perform the action, but his whole body and soul inform the result.

I was cut off from the world in my mighty fortress but after a while word reached me that my colleague in Wittenberg, Dr Karlstadt, had rushed ahead with his own reforms. At Christmas that year, the year I was sentenced to death, he changed the service of Mass, abolished the elevation of the host, distributed communion in both kinds of bread and wine. He performed the ceremony in lay clothes, and to great publicity married a peasant girl some days later. He denounced images and pictures and stirred up the townsfolk to demolish and burn them. He threw aside his priestly and academic robes and began to wear a peasant's smock. I had to leave the safety of Wartburg castle to sort out the chaos.

(*Pause.*)

Man is often distinguished by his folly, and fools are sometimes indistinguishable from their masters. Emperor Maximilian's court fool, Kunz von der Rosen, was a good example. He tethered a fat pig to a stake in the market place, assembled the blind people of the town, handed each of them a club and promised the pig to the one who killed it. To roars of laughter from the princes and people, the blind, mad with greed, clubbed each other viciously in a long and bloody fight. A macabre allegory of our times.

It was also during that solitary time in the Wartburg that I struggled with the devil. Very often I felt myself to be in the presence of Satan in an incarnate form. I was especially plagued by him at night. Once he was so threatening I threw my inkpot at him. (*He leers into the darkness.*) To me he was the spirit of melancholy, like Saul whose evil spirit David had to drive away by playing the harp. It is the devil who entices people to commit suicide. I have always had one or two devils who keep a close watch on me ... very purposeful devils they are. And when they can make no headway with my heart they attack my mind and torment me that way. (*To Stranger*) And when they come again I'm going to grab them and stick them up my arse. (*To audience*) That's where he belongs.

I had many enemies. I owed my life to the Elector Frederick. He was called "the Wise". Frederick the Cautious would have been a better description. The poor man did his duty in condemning my teachings, but then it was he who quietly let me be quietly smuggled out of reach of the Church.

I was indeed a troublesome monk. He was proud of his collection of relics and the indulgences they gathered. I had preached about them in his presence, and got into his bad graces for doing so. In the very Castle Church where I posted my theses condemning indulgences he kept his collection, 5,005 relics in all, each listed with its appropriate indulgence. Devout contemplation of the whole collection could earn a person 1,443 years remission of purgatory. It included such treasures as a piece of straw from the manger, one of the Blessed Virgin's hairs and a drop of her milk. There was a complete corpse of one of the children murdered by Herod in Bethlehem.

But he was no fool. He didn't agree with me, but defended my right to teach what I believed.

He wasn't the only one to collect relics.

Archbishop Albrecht of Mainz – I should say Cardinal - when he needed money, announced a new indulgence based on recently found relics he had acquired. These included the basin in which Pilate washed his hands; St Christopher's shoulder blade; some of the manna in the wilderness; twigs from the burning bush; and a piece of the very earth from which Adam was created. The catalogue promised 8,993 fragments and 42 complete bodies of saints; the indulgence was calculated at 39,245,120 years and 220 days. I replied to the Archbishop's announcement with a thunderbolt addressed to his Grace himself. I told him he should leave the poor people alone and not mislead and rob them.

Then I drew up a list of my own of further possible items for his collection. These included: three flames from the burning bush upon Mount Sinai; five fine bright chords from David's harp; one long hair from the beard of Beelzebub; half a wing from St Gabriel the Archangel; two feathers and one egg from the Holy Ghost.

There were many more, I told him, where they came from.

(*His smile fades, he comes forward to look again into the darkness.*)

(*To stranger*) Are you still there? If you are still there you will be waiting for me to say something about the peasants. Whom they said I betrayed.

(*Pause.*)

The peasants' war was the darkest period of my life. When they rose in revolt, was it because of my teachings? My enemies claimed that. These poor people, their rights had been eaten away over the centuries. Poverty, hunger, hardship were everywhere. Revolt was inevitable. At first we knew little of what was happening outside our own area, but rumours began to reach us of atrocities committed by the peasants. It was then I turned away from them. They were invoking the authority of my teachings to justify their crimes, and committing atrocities in my name, thinking I would support them. I had encouraged them only to free themselves from spiritual tyranny. What I had written against the Church and the hierarchy led many peasants to believe I would support their attacks on their rulers. On a journey through towns in our area I became enraged at what I saw: the widespread burning of convents, monasteries, bishops' palaces, libraries. Their leader, Thomas Müntzer, became for me the spirit of evil, Satan himself. I condemned the violence as the devil's work, railed against them as thieves and assassins. I called on the nobles to put down the rebels like mad dogs. They deserved death in body and soul as highwaymen and murderers. Rebellion is intolerable and at any moment the world could have been destroyed.

But I condemned the princes and rulers with the same vehemence that I opposed the peasants. When I heard how they had been so savagely suppressed, I stormed against the nobility who had treated these poor people with such extreme cruelty.

I had only one yardstick, the word of God. I measured peasants and princes alike against it. And as for Münzer, a visionary, a dreamer, the poor man was tortured in the most horrifying way and executed.

And ... if I am to confess what are called my excesses I must also speak of the Jews.

I was convinced that if they heard our preaching, and how we revere the Old Testament, many of them might be won over. Jesus Christ was born a Jew, I said. Jews are of the lineage of Christ, blood relations, cousins and brothers of Our Lord. But nothing could persuade them that our Jesus was the Messiah. Instead they had crucified Him.

I desired profoundly to convert them. When they persisted in their blindness I turned violently against them, called for them to be driven from our presence, lest we be contaminated by their abominable vices and blasphemy, earning God's wrath and being damned along with them.

I called for their synagogues to be burned down as schools of lies; if Moses lived he'd be the first to torch them. Tear down their houses, I said, lest they teach at home. Take away their books, forbid their rabbis to teach. Better that we tear the tongues out of their throats than hear their denial of Christ. We were at fault in not slaying them.

But if they had only been willing to be converted from their blasphemy then we would gladly, gladly have forgiven them.

After so much pain, I ask again: was there room for love in my life other than for Christ our Lord? And my beloved wife Kate and our dear children.

Whom else have I really loved?

My Prior, Father Staupitz. He was my superior in the Lord, my teacher and my father. A man who was too humble where I was too proud. Even when he disagreed with me I could not condemn him. When the time came for us to go our separate ways he still called me his "dearest Martin", and recalled the Bible story of David's love for Jonathan and his lament at the death of his friend:

"I am distressed for thee, my brother Jonathan: very pleasant hast thou been unto me: thy love to me was wonderful, passing the love of woman."

The final words he spoke to me were:

"Perhaps my spirit has been too timid. You must understand, Martin, if I hide myself in silence."

And so our friendship ended in stillness and tranquillity. Shortly afterwards he died. I was left with the memory of quiet conversations under the pear tree.

And poor Tetzel. My first and bitterest enemy, I had started out by wanting to knock a hole in his drum. Only a year later he was ill in Leipzig. That was during all the excitement of the disputation in that city, when my life was at stake. Condemned and abandoned by his former friends in Rome, he lay rejected, ignored, broken and alone. I wrote a gentle letter to the poor man as he lay dying, told him he was not to take the blame on himself. He had not fathered the scandal, merely been a victim, a scapegoat.

What else is there left for me to declare?

My great weariness?

My bitter agony at the loss of my darling daughter Magdalena just three years ago on the edge of womanhood? When she died I sent an angel to heaven.

My despair when I looked around me in the past years and saw, despite all my strivings, that people have shown no desire for a change in their hearts.

Those who are faithful call themselves Lutheran. What is Luther? This teaching is not mine. What have I done, poor, stinking sack of worms that I am, that Christ's children should be called after my unholy name? No, dear friends, I told them, let us have done with partisan names and call ourselves Christians, after Him whose teachings we have.

I even thought of leaving Wittenberg, longed to go back to the places of my childhood. Wittenberg has never been home to me. I remained a pilgrim and wanderer there, even in my faith and teaching. When the counts of Mansfeld called on me once again to resolve their dispute, despite my infirmity – and despite Kate's worries about my undertaking a long and hazardous winter journey - I gladly returned here to where I grew up. I even feel myself to be a Mansfelder once more. And, thanks be to the good God, the counts are reconciled and are at peace.

Oh, Kate, Kate. I thought of you and the young ones today when I heard the cheerful sound of sleigh bells outside my window, and the laughter of the young children of the counts as they passed by celebrating the reconciliation.

But the days of laughter are gone. I have worked myself to death. For one man, I have done enough. I will go lie down in the earth now and sleep. It is over for me, except (*he takes up his staff*) ... except for just another little thwack still at the pope.

(*He clutches staff, smiling.*)

One final thwack at His Holiness? Yes? My last.

(He drops staff, turns slowly to look to picture of Christ , then at books. Turns to look up into light.)

You have come for me. At last.

(Bows head.)

I am ready to be judged. What I have done well. What I have done ill.

(*Music: Agnus Dei from Palestrina's* Missa Papae Marcelli.)

It has been a long wait. I am not afraid.

(He looks up, smiling.)

I am ready.

CURTAIN

Luther - Chronology

1483	Luther born in Eisleben.
1484	Family moves to Mansfeld.
	Swiss reformer Zwingli born.
1491	Henry VIII born.
1493	Cesare Borgia becomes cardinal.
1497	Da Vinci completes *Last Supper.*
1500	Michelangelo completes *Pietà.*
1500-04	University at Erfurt.
1505	Becomes Augustinian monk.
1506	Columbus dies.
	Da Vinci paints *Mona Lisa.*
1507	Ordained priest.
1510-11	Journey to Rome.
1511	Swiss reformer Calvin born.
1512-13	Professor, 'tower' insight on grace.
1516-17	Tetzel sent to Germany.
1516	Erasmus Greek *New Testament.*
1517	Posts theses (Eve of Feast of All Saints)
1518	1st letter to Pope.
	To Augsburg to face Cajetan.
1519	2nd letter to Pope.
	Charles V elected emperor.
	Debates in Leipzig with Eck.
1520	Bull Exsurge Domine.
	Burns Decretals and Bull.
1521	Diet of Worms. *Here I stand* (Emperor Charles V).
1521	Luther excommunicated by Leo XII. Taken by Elector Frederick, to Wartburg Castle, Eisenach.
	Karlstadt's "reforms".
	Edict of Worms.
	Death of Josquin des Prez.
1522	Returns to Wittenberg to sort out Karlstadt problem.
1524	Stopped wearing habit.
	Remained monk, no longer in Order.
1525	Married (he was 42).
	Peasants' Revolt.
	Elector Frederick dies.
1526	First child, Hans.
1527	Machiavelli dies.
1530	Luther in Coburg.
	Imperial Diet of Augsburg.
1534	Luther's translation of Old Testament.
1535	Thomas More beheaded.
1530-46	Years of family, organisation and politics, illnesses.
1542	Daughter Magdalena dies.
1543	Anti-Semitic tracts.
1545	Council of Trent convoked.
	Albrecht of Mainz dies.
	Luther: vitriolic tract against the papacy.
1546	Death of Luther in Eisleben.

www.ingramcontent.com/pod-product-compliance
Ingram Content Group UK Ltd.
Pitfield, Milton Keynes, MK11 3LW, UK
UKHW020230250726
13967UKWH00001B/285